THE BEAUTY OF BEING

Free

ATIYA

ATIYA'S LIGHT PUBLISHING

ATIYA'S LIGHT

PUBLISHING

ARIZONA   CARIBBEAN   CHICAGO   LONDON

Atiya's Light Publishing
www.atiyaslight.com
info@atiyaslight.com

Library of Congress Control Number: 2014940233
ISBN: 978-0-9916444-2-1

Cover Photo By: Ingram Jones

Printed in the United States of America

Dedicated to the ones who seek to live life to the fullest being fantastically themselves without apology!

Acknowledgments

This is a gift for my fellow travelers on the path to enlightenment and those in search of life, liberty, and the pursuit of happiness. Many thanks to my husband, children, family, friends, teachers, spiritual guides, and strangers who have encouraged and supported me along the way.

I am grateful for you being there during times I needed it the most. You know who you are. Also, a special thank you to those whose intentions may not have been well-intended, for you too have played a vital role in helping me to break free from limiting belief systems, the chains of oppression and suppression. You served as a catalyst for me living and loving me for who I am. You too know who you are.

Boxes are for packing things away, putting them up somewhere for when and if you should decide to use them again. There is not a box that can contain me or my reason for being. Universal love has no season, it's eternal.

I trust you will enjoy reading this book and gain some valuable insights to become a better, more loving, and freer YOU!

Foreword

Strength has many definitions. It is the intrinsic quality of the divine soul that causes (what is not believed to possess the ability), to overcome all obstacles that impair progress. It is the eternal source of Light that guides the blind to the dawn of freedom. Strength is Eternal and unpossessed of any, yet it is seen in all things. It is the meek slave woman who accomplishes the unthinkable; it is the Hebrew child born to rule; it is the patience to outlive oppressors; it is the overturning of systems in the blink of an eye. Strength is knowing innately what no one else believes, and manifesting it before disbelieving eyes. It is tied to faith in the unseen. As the sperm knows of no world beyond the egg, and the fetus that it becomes, knows nothing beyond the womb; as the child loves their Mother, strength is the constant breaking through the known into the unknown and learning to master what is completely new.

This is a brief walk into the realm of the unexplored self. On the other side is a better "you"; free from anxiety, fear and grief. Take this journey and mount up on the wings of discovery of what has been inside of you, all along.

Atiya has the rare ability to articulate what we know deep inside, but we never say to ourselves. Her words are a doorway to a mirror; one in which each is able to see the best part of us. This simple Truth can be said in the most eloquent manner, and the gentle delivery brings ease to the mind and heart. Listen with your soul and you will feel elevated, as you read. May you be blessed to transcend to your Highest Self.

Amin Shabazz Muhammad
Practitioner of the Martial & Healing Arts
Professional in Information Technology & Coding
U.S.A.

Table of Contents

Introduction

There are many symbols of freedom as there are many levels of it. However on the road to freedom, often times one's liberty comes with the help of others. That assistance is sometimes overt while in other cases it is masked requiring an astute mind and heart to use the power of intuition and discernment to unlock its mysteries. At any junction, the bells of freedom have a beautiful sound - a sound that resounds in the hearts of persons who for far too long have only dreamed of its reality. Yet freedom is an ever present truth to which you only must recognize that it is there, simply waiting for you to embrace it, and live according to its creed.

Harriet Tubman was a second-generation slave. This means that her parents were slaves and she too as a result was confined by physical slavery. Yet Harriet Tubman had a mind and heart set on freedom. She knew that no form of physical captivity could ever conquer and bring her mind and heart into subjection. She understood all too well her birthright and no amount of corporeal intimidation or persuasion could ever dominate her mental or emotional capacity for freedom. She was in fact free, and soon many others came to understand the power and beauty of her freedom.

Harriet Tubman could not be held by physical bondage, because she had a mind that was free and a will determined in freedom. She escaped the reality of slavery and made over nineteen trips back to the south to retrieve others. She never lost a slave, nor did she ever fail in her mission. Further, she was willing to take a life that dared to have the audacity to impede freedom. She was faithful to freedom, was unwavering for freedom's sake and just as Moses led the children of Israel out of Egypt, so it is that Harriet Tubman used the North Star as a guide to lead hundreds of slaves out of captivity.

Rosa Parks inspired the Montgomery Bus Boycott not because she was the first to refuse to give up her seat. She was considered the "Mother of the Freedom Movement" because of the season and time in which she took a stand or in her case a seat. She refused to continue giving in to conditions that were in contrary to life, liberty, and the pursuit of happiness. Rosa asserted that the more you give in and comply with oppressive conditions, the more oppressive it becomes.

Freedom is a mindset. No form of subjugation can contain a free mind - one that is conscious and aware. To break the chains of oppression of any kind is to first break the shackles of mental bondage, which can color your perception of reality and greatly impact your ability to be productive and a consequential force in the world. This is why the first act of freedom is a renewed mind. One can more readily comprehend this with the story of the flea and the elephant.

Both the elephant and the flea were captured in their youth. Under normal conditions, the flea can jump about eighteen inches high. However, if you put a flea in a jar and close the lid, the flea may start out attempting to jump its normal height, but once it is stopped by the lid of the jar, it ceases to jump to its ability even after the lid has been removed. The same is true with the elephant.

A young elephant that has been chained down for several years with a big ball and chain will naturally make several attempts to break free. After the exertion of trying repeatedly with no success, the elephant submits to a life of being yoked to the ball and chain. Over time, the elephant grows up and the ball and chains are replaced with a small thin rope. The adult elephant has the ability and the strength to break the rope to free itself, yet it remains bound and will not break free because it does not know its own strength and ability. It doesn't' recognize its power because it was conditioned to believe it had none. Therefore, the elephant as big and strong as it is, remains tied up.

The elephant and the flea, like many people during slavery, accepted a condition that was totally contrary to their natural ability and calling. The same thing happens today. Until and unless there is a realization and recognition of the truth, faulty reasoning will continue to exist and keep you locked outside of your purpose. It has been documented that Harriet Tubman once stated that she freed over one thousand slaves, but she could have freed a thousand more if they knew that they were slaves.

Sometimes it takes someone outside of yourself to drive you to freedom. Likewise, a person who has been mentally bound all of their life, are not aware perhaps that they are not living in freedom and thus goes from one form of bondage to another, thinking that they are actually free. In order for them to become conscious of the fact that they are not free, they must taste the wine of freedom and that can only come about by a restored mind. The mental chains must be removed and a new way of thinking must arise.

Harriet Tubman used what became known as the "underground railroad" to free slaves in her day. It was not an actual physical railroad, but a network of people and places designed to aid a slave's journey to freedom. It was considered underground because a person's path was often treaded without observation thus without resistance. One's freedom today is very much the same.

There are guides to help us recognize and board a modern day "underground railroad." Their manner is very delicate and refined as to require one to elevate their vibrations, level of thinking, and consciousness in order to imbibe the exquisite ethereal beauty of it all. There is no song, writing, or painting that fails to hint at or reveal some essence of the truth, and only those who are consciously aware can recognize it for what it is.

It's time to wake up, wake up, wake up. You have been dormant and in an inactive state of existence for far too long. You are free! You have only been limited by your own state of mind. As I would say to the flea, "the lid is off of the jar, you can jump the eighteen inches;" or the elephant, "You have the strength and ability to break the ropes that confine you." The same I say to you, "Your inability to move is only a condition that is caused by your way of thinking, so renew your mind to restore your condition."

Harriet Tubman may have been physically confined, yet her mind and heart was anything but. Because of the level of her thinking, regardless as to her inability to read or write, she ultimately changed her physical reality because of her mindset. She was cognizant and aware of her situation and determined it was not based on the truth. Harriet knew the truth. She knew that freedom belonged to her; in fact she was freedom and acted upon the truth of who she was. You see, knowledge is not just power, it is your ticket to freedom.

I am here to help you elevate your level of awareness and consciousness. My goal is to inspire you to find your creative genius, discover, and tap into your divine gifts as you pursue happiness and self-determination.

My mission, vision and life's work is to innovatively and intuitively empower, build and maximize human potential by inspiring profound transformation in the thinking and behavior towards life, with the intent and purpose of helping you to realize your dreams and achieve joy, success and fulfillment in life. Only when you understand and know who you are can you built like relationships.

This message is one of freedom and about basking in the beauty and power of being totally free. While freedom to you may come from having the symbols of success, meaning fine homes and cars, a large bank account or more, real freedom begins in the mind and transcends what you may have amassed or will gain materially or physically.

Be blessed as you continue your path to enlightenment. Enjoy the ride!

Chapter 1

Understanding Real and Authentic Freedom

Freedom is a multiplicate term. Simplistically, it is having the power or liberty to determine one's own actions without restraint. However, to understand real and authentic freedom is a much deeper exploration. The word freedom is actually "free + dome." The word dome comes from the Latin root domus which means house. It is also a hemispherical roof or vault. A vault is an underground chamber used for safekeeping valuables. It comes from the Latin root voltare which means to turn or leap.

A roof is the highest point or uppermost part of a house or structure. Hemispherical means either of the two halves of the celestial sphere lying north or south of the celestial equator. So when hemispherical roof is mentioned, it is drawing reference to the north point of the sphere. Sphere simply means hollow space. Now, it has been said that you are the real house of God. A house is a dwelling place or shelter. The term "god" means to call, invoke, or pour. Pour comes from the Latin root purare which means to purify. Call means to give a name to, visit, or literally to stand at the door and call. Therefore if you are the house of God, this means that God lives in you.

Let's go a little deeper. We have established that you are in fact the house of God. So, now, the hemispherical roof or vault of the house of God is the uppermost or top of your body, which directs you to the top of your head. However, dome also means to cover and vault is an underground chamber. Therefore, your dome is your mind. Mind means memory, remembrance, or thought. In its root it means prophet. The verb prophet means to speak, while the noun prophet is an interpreter or spokesperson. Are you following what I am saying to you thus far? Listen to that inner voice.

Let's go deeper into free. Free simply means being able to act at will without being under compulsion or restraint to do so. It is to be without obstruction or impediment. However, when you examine the meaning of free a little closer, in its root it means joyful, beloved, noble, and friend; yet more importantly free means love.

Harriet Tubman used the "North Star" as a guide to freedom. To Native Americans the North Star is referred to as the fire star or the Great Chief in the Sky. While it is not the brightest star, the North Star is one of the most significant stars because it is reliable for guidance. What makes it reliable is because of its outstanding quality of its location. The North Star is recognized as a symbol of stability, leadership, and guardianship.

We live in a multidimensional universe. Behind every physical reality is a spiritual reality and there are many layers and meanings to various things. While Harriet Tubman may have used the physical North Star or Polaris to guide herself and others to freedom, what is more significant is that she used her ability to think, problem solve, the knowledge of herself, the love for self and her people to influence motion. It was her destiny as it is yours to be free. Your birthright or "true nature" is to be free. You are free and that was the original idea or thought. You are the prophet of your own destiny and it is up to you to deliver the message, because you are the one called to rule and lead.

The Underground Railroad that Harriet Tubman used may have been a network of people and places, however, substantively speaking the Underground Railroad that Harriet Tubman used was the power of her own mind to think and see beyond her own physical reality to manifest her vision and the reality of freedom. It was underground because the power of who she truly was had been hidden beneath the surface and kept secret until the proper time and season. Her ability to guide came from her acknowledgement of her freedom and thus lent itself to her being able to provide an open way for others to travel between the two points of the most important journey – the journey from bondage to freedom. Yet, it was her conviction to do what she had been called to do. The call came from the God within herself. The ideas that she believed to be true were in fact her truth and in her action she roared, "I believe, therefore I am!"

There is a passage in the biblical scripture in Luke which provides an illustration of a very important principle. One day Jesus was praying. After finishing prayer, one of his disciples said, "Lord, teach us how to pray as John taught his disciples." Jesus responded by saying pray on this wise, "Our Father which art in heaven, Hallowed be thy name. Thy kingdom come. Thy will be done, on earth as it is in heaven... Now, Jesus means savior. A savior is one who delivers or rescues another. Lord means keeper of the house. He was able to walk in authority, with influence and mastery because he acknowledged who he was and walked within the context of that understanding. His anointing came from his recognition and acceptance of He who was in him was much greater than he who was in the world. Jesus knew who he was and walked in the light of who he was. He made no excuses for it.

When the disciples asked Jesus how to pray, in essence what they were asking was for Jesus to teach them how to negotiate effectively to receive the same respect and honor that he was receiving among them. Jesus pretty much told them that it was up to them to choose and manifest their inspired ideas from their own mind into the world and that the essential quality of their idea would be determined by the wholeness of it and whether or not they were actually being true to whom they were. In the parable of the Good Samaritan when asked about the law, Jesus said, "Love the Lord your God with all your heart, soul, strength, and mind; and love your neighbor as yourself." Jesus went on to say, "If you do this, you will live."

Now what Jesus was actually saying was the way to measure or guide is to demonstrate and prove the service of your own calling and reason for being born. He was encouraging them to do so wholly and without limit and to be courageous to breathe life into it with force, power and moral resistance when necessary, to live and walk in your purpose, and sanction or permit others to do the same. If you do this you will experience joy. If you do this you will be free. You are called to exercise your free agency. You are a free agent. This is what Harriet Tubman did, this is what

Jesus did, and this is what you must do to experience the real beauty and joy of living.

In essence, real and authentic freedom is the love for self and the love for humanity.

Chapter 2

Transforming Through the Breath of Universal Love

We discussed the first act of freedom being a renewed mind. The second act of freedom is a heart filled with love. "Universal Love is a higher vibration and the source of all healing. It elevates and sharpens your intuitive signals and helps to increase awareness, establish balance, and maintain a harmonic existence. To love is to live."

Universal love gives you total freedom. Enlightenment comes through the channels of loving intentions. When you turn your attention toward the concept of one rotation or revolution around one central point – that one central point being love, there will be peace and harmony and inevitably everything in creation will fit together. Love cultivates joy because they are one in the same.

There is no competition with a universal mindset because it is a knowing that there is a constant flow of abundance more than sufficient for all living creatures, the whole of humanity, and the entire multidimensional reality. With this awareness comes the realization that there is no longer the need to struggle against or oppose another. To antagonize someone else is to contradict self. Likewise, to give to one is not to deny another. Universal love takes into consideration the dominion of every human being and their right to free agency and self-governance. However, this is only fulfilled in an environment where there is real love and oneness.

People hinder and block others out of fear. Fear provokes, distresses, and upsets balance. Its wrath produces everything in contrary to love. To transform through the breath of universal love is to be a source of happiness and delight. One does this by taking in (inhaling) loving energies and sending out (exhaling) loving energies. When competing forces arise, no need to resist them, understand that everything has a polar opposite and when confronted with anything directly opposite in character or tendency to that of love, simply send out more loving energy as this will balance out fear or the competing force. Remember, the significance of the North Star is its positioning or location.

Interestingly enough, although the cardinal direction of North looking at a map or compass is up or at the top, the word itself means down or under. What makes the North Star positioning or location key is the fact that it is near the North Celestial Pole. All the stars that can be seen from the Northern Hemisphere rotate at the point of the North Celestial Pole. The earth rotates on its axis 1,037 1/3 miles per hour. The earth's axis is an imaginary straight line which intersects an imaginary sphere of a gigantic beam of light centered through the earth at two points (north and south). The two points are what is referred to as celestial pole.

The axis is actually the pivot point or the beam of balance and as the earth spins it is tilted on its axis and has a wobble. It wobbles because of the gravitational forces of the Sun and the Moon, and to some degree other bodies in motion. The equator is the imaginary line that forms a big circle around the earth and divides it into the Northern and Southern Hemispheres. The equator is the equalizer of the day and night. An equalizer counterbalances opposing forces. If you look at a diagram of the positioning of the celestial poles, the equator, and the tilt of the earth, it would resemble a tilted cross. The North Celestial Pole would be above the Northern Hemisphere. This is the area where the North Star Polaris is located.

In observing Polaris, what is viewed as a single point of light is in truth three stars. The primary star Polaris (A) is six times the mass of the sun. Now, Polaris has not always been the North Star. Likewise, it will not always be the North Star. For example, during the time of the ancient Egyptians and the building of the pyramids, Thuban in the constellation of Draco or also known as Alpha Draconis was the North Star. Although it lies in the Dragon's tail, the name is Arabic for "serpent's head." This star can be seen from the bottom of the central passage of Cheops – the Great Pyramid.

The Future North Star is Errai or Alrai (Gamma Ce-
phei). It is a binary star which is two stars revolving around
a common center of mass. The name derives from Arabic
and means "the shepherd." This future "King" North Star,
which is one of the brightest in the constellation Cepheus,
does not come alone. It can be recognized by the striking
and lasting shine of its companion star or "Queen," which
has a mass about 0.409 times that of the Sun. Errai shines as
a circumpolar star. A circumpolar star is one that never sets
or disappears below the horizon. The word horizon means
to separate or divide. Please listen carefully and listen to
your inner voice.

The present North Star, Polaris, means "dog's tail" and
has been around for a while, even during the time the
Europeans sailed across the Atlantic. The North Star is a
beacon of light and holds a fixed position in the sky. It fades
and brightens over a four-day period. It is said that in
addition to the Cepheid stars, there are two other stars and
an unseen object orbiting Polaris.

The point is this; we are at a turning point in the consciousness of human awareness and therefore must vibrate according to that higher level of consciousness. When all beings move through universal love, peace and harmony exists. Therefore, allow love and light to flow freely through you as a prismatic reflector and manifestation of the Infinite Source. The process of discovery begins within the hidden treasure of your being. Open the channels to universal love and begin the exquisite journey to total alignment. The path of enlightenment leads to an awakening and realization that the greatest warrior is one who is able to maintain peace.

Transforming through the breath of universal love is a way to heal, become free, and gain mastery in your life. Oxygen is the most important element needed to take a journey to higher planes. It is important for you to breathe.

The biblical scripture says, "Then the LORD God formed a man from the dust of the ground and breathed into his nostrils the breath of life, and the man became a living being." What this actually means is that during a time when you find you have been reduced to poverty, call on your power and ability to create a mental picture in your mind to shape your destiny and turn your condition around. All it takes is for you to realize that, even in your ignorance and senselessness and in the absence of you not having everything you may need at the moment, you can fill the void. Get up early in the morning and get busy manifesting your idea and the picture in your mind to change your condition or state of affairs.

To be senseless is to be devoid of purpose and lack intelligence. If you do not have purpose in your life or reason for being, then you are empty and have not the faculty of understanding or the power of discernment and your material environment will reflect your state of your mind. To have purpose is to have an aim and intentions for being. What is your reason for living and getting up everyday? Your purpose in life is your will to live. It's what you think to put forth or aim at. To aim is to blow or in other words to breathe.

Oxygen is the most abundant element in the earth's crust. It is essential for life. The word comes from the

Greek root oxys which means sharp, and from the French root gene which means something that produces and from the Greek root genes meaning creation or formation. The first and most basic principle here is to be conscious of whom you are and be yourself in all boldness to maintain your livelihood. No one can tell you who you are. That is something that you must settle on your own. However, when you do decide, function in that particular way to gain mastery. Live well, be of superior character, establish oneness, profit and share in the rewards of the earth's abundance.

Have you heard the phrase, "being full of life?" Well, being full of life is being full of Prana - life's vital energy. Prana is universal energy. Energy is force of expression. Expression is the act of manifesting. Energy does not just exist, it flows. To flow is to well forth or circulate. Circulate is to move in a circle or revolve. When we breathe in and out, the energy that manifests itself through the process of breathing in and out is prana, not the breath itself.

Breathing like everything in the universe has two polarities: Breath in and breath out. As discussed earlier, polarity is contrasting tendencies or principles. With respect to polar opposition, poles are different aspects of the same event. They are not two different things, but rather opposite sides of the same coin. In other words, one end of a pole is directly opposite in character and tendency, yet there is only one pole.

Yin and Yang symbolize two opposite principles in nature like the moon and the sun. While they are opposites, they are both a part of nature and both play a significant role in balance. When one is stronger the other is weaker. They are not Yin and Yang alone; meaning they contain parts of the other and one cannot exist without the other. Yin is feminine and represents the unseen or subjective reality. Yin draws you into your center and can represent the breath in or inhalation. Yang is masculine and represents the seen or objective reality. Yang pulls you away from your center and can represent the breath out or exhalation. Polarity is important to equilibrium.

"Accept your own and be yourself" is a Yin and Yang expression. In essence it means to receive what you have been given and give what you have to give. It means to exchange. Yin and Yang, breathing, the moon and the sun are all manifestations of wobbling. So the earth's wobble is the principle of exchanging or going back and forth. Its tilt on the axis is representative of leaning on each other when we need support.

Understanding Prana is the gateway to consciousness. Physically speaking, if you did not get enough oxygen, you could lose consciousness. Well, the same rings true with prana and awareness. As we travel the journey toward enlightenment, it is essential to expand our minds and hearts. Universal love allows us a deeper understanding and acceptance of truth. It allows us to think consciously and creatively and to flow freely. The Serenity Prayer is a very good reminder of the importance of universal love and balance.

"God grant me the serenity to accept the things I cannot change, courage to change the things I can, and wisdom to know the difference."

At the core, this inquiry is a calling to your consciousness to provide clarity to help you receive from others what is for you to have and to be of the mind and thoughts to know and be able to make the distinction of what should be measured to others. Universal love is a higher vibration, higher state of awareness, and a higher consciousness. To function properly in this realm, we must balance ourselves and abound in love.

Chapter 3

Breaking Through the Impediments to Free Agency

To break through the impediments to free agency is to overcome competing forces for the greater good; and move beyond that which attempts to hinder your happiness and success. You do this by continuing to work effectively. To work effectively is to continue to be productive regardless as to the opposing force. One can accomplish this by understanding polarity and actively operating in love and according to degree.

A degree is a step or unit of rotation. It is a unit of measurement expressing the amount, the extent, the level of intensity, or position of something that happens or is present. To measure is to ascertain relative value or amount according to a given standard. The universal law of relativity deals with space and time and states that all things are relative and exists only by reference of something else.

What this simply means is that hot is only hot because of cold. One would not know hot to be hot without them knowing cold to be cold, and depending on their frame of reference hot may be cold and cold may be hot. For example, a person who lives on the continent of Africa may visit Chicago during a time when it is 55-degrees Fahrenheit. To that person, it may be considered cold. However, for another person who lives on the continent of Antarctica, 55-degrees Fahrenheit may be hot. You see, hot and cold are relative and how you view 55-degrees depends on your point of reference.

Other examples include big and small, tall and short, fast and slow, and so forth. Things just are what they are. We give them significance and purpose, and the meaning we give to them depends on our point of reference. In terms of breaking through the impediments to free agency, when presented with an opposing force, your aim or purpose for being must be the standard, the focal point of attention, point of concentration of interest, or in other words the pole.

Remember a pole is the axis of a sphere. Your purpose in life must be your turn around point which reflects importance as you navigate through life. In other words you are the sphere, your purpose is the axis, and your ability to accurately measure and move according to degree is what equalizes the competing forces. Balance is essential because it harmonizes two opposing forces. To the degree of which opposition comes is to the degree of what you must put out in order to equalize, harmonize, or reconcile your situation.

As you examine the eagle, it demonstrates equilibrium in its flight and how to bring two opposing forces into agreement. An eagle is known for its ability to soar high, its sharp vision, and amazing strength. While its wings may span over eight feet, its body weight may be barely the weight of a domestic cat. The power of the eagle lies in its wings and its jaw. The muscles used for flying make up for about half of the eagle's body weight.

As an eagle flies, it flaps its wings to increase the flow of air over the top of its wings helping it to rise. However, at times, the eagle uses natural flowing forces in the atmosphere to fly higher. To increase or decrease speed, an eagle only needs to change the position of its wings. It gains the most power for flight in the downward stroke of the wings.

To comprehend how an eagle flies, there are certain terms that are important to understand. They are: Relative wind, lift, drag, and thrust. Relative wind is airflow relative to the eagle. It is created by the movement of the eagle as it flaps its wings and flies through the air. Relative wind is exactly opposite to the direction that the eagle is flying and equal in magnitude.

Lift is the force that directly opposes the weight of the eagle. It is what helps to keep the eagle in the air. The eagle's weight is important with respect to gravity. Gravity is the power or force of attraction between two masses. Because of gravity, the weight of the eagle will always cause an inclination toward the center of the earth. However, to create lift and overcome weight force, the eagle flaps its wings to create an opposing force. If the eagle did not flap its wings, it would not get off the ground, because where there is no motion, there is no lift. You must work to elevate your condition and to rise.

Drag is the resistive force that opposes the eagle's flight through the air and makes it difficult for the eagle to move quickly. As the eagle flies, the air resists the eagle's motion. So, another way to look at drag is as air resistance. Air is atmosphere. As you take action or work to do something or bring something about, whether you want to or not, you impact things around you. It's a natural occurrence. Yet, like an eagle, you can use drag to your benefit. When an eagle wants to slow down and land, it uses drag.

When an eagle wants to overcome drag, it uses the strength and power of its wings to push or propel itself forward. This action produces another force. Thrust is the force generated by the wings to move the eagle through the air. When you want to speed up or move forward at an accelerated rate, it's necessary to push harder by working more effectively and efficiently.

An eagle is presented with two challenges in its quest to fly. First, it must overcome its weight by any opposing force. Second, it must control itself while in flight. Both of these difficulty factors are related to weight and location – the eagle's weight and the center of gravity. Both weight and the center of gravity are changing variables. Therefore, an eagle must constantly make adjustments in order to maintain balance.

Look at it this way. Lift pushes the eagle up, weight pulls it down, thrust makes it go forward, and drag slows it down. All four forces are needed for flight to happen. Consider the lift in your life as the help that comes along the way on your journey. Weight is the internal weaknesses of yourself that consistently pulls you down. Thrust is your purpose and what should be your consistent course of action. Drag is the obstacles or annoyances that come along which can slow down your progress if you allow it.

Stress weighs you down. Unnecessary burdens weigh you down. Some people can weigh you down. Unresolved issues weigh you down. Your hands are like the eagle's wings. You have power to turn your situation around and move any opposing forces out of your way, by making necessary adjustments moving forward with courage and strength.

As the eagle demonstrates, size has nothing to do with its strength and ability to soar. It is efficient and its wings represent balance of energies. What this means is that the eagle is very capable of producing a desired result, and so are you!

The eagle's wings represent the ability to move swiftly and accomplish goals and objectives. Just as an eagle can balance the speed of flight by the positioning of its wings, you too can balance your life by the position you take or by the degree of your action. Your ingenuity in rising above the energy that is in motion which affects you or moves in contrary to what you are working toward is the lesson in the eagle's flight. The eagle can fly higher than any bird and thus is said to be considered a messenger of the Creator. You are the creator, and the creator is you. Your aptitude to create is directly relative to your altitude.

An eagle has keen vision. This is representative of intuition and power of perception. You must be able to see beyond what is in order to see what you envision. Just as the eagle uses its sight to discern, swoop down, and capture its prey, you must put things in proper perspective; stay focused, and remain steadfast to seize the object of your aim. The eagle's feet and talons are said to be stronger than a human hand and their jaw can crush animals in mid-flight. The strength of this amazing bird is representative of the fortitude and courage with which you must walk in your purpose and not allow opposing forces to hinder your rise.

Once in the air, it becomes easier to fly. Thus, the biblical scripture of Isaiah states, "But those who hope in the LORD will renew their strength. They will soar on wings like eagles; they will run and not grow weary, they will walk and not be faint."

Chapter 4

Gaining the Courage to Live Freely

Often times when we are younger, people, especially those who are close to us have a tendency to steal our dreams. You may have one or two who believe in you, but for the most part, the majority does not see or recognize who you really are.

As a result, you may not get the necessary help and support you need in order to fly. Yet, after a long journey, sometimes twenty years or longer, a voice speaks more clearly into your consciousness and louder than ever before. The voice has always been there, it has just been there inside waiting on the right moment to come forth.

Almost overnight, something happens, and you start to awaken to something that you may have felt before, but not as strong. All of a sudden, it pushes itself forward and through an awakening experience and through a pressure that before you could not handle, it finally comes forth - the birth of a brand new you.

Sometimes living in your purpose can be challenging because people do not always understand why you move the way you do. Family is usually the ones who find it difficult to see the person you are becoming because they have been used to the person you were. In their mind they often see what was as opposed to what is. So they miss out on a magical process – A miracle in the making.

Sometimes you have to fire people that are in your life to give them the message that you are just as important as they are and have just as much a right to self-determination as they do. You fire them by no longer allowing them the privilege of sharing your space.

Harriet Tubman was determined to experience the joy and happiness of freedom. Yet to do so she had to go through the pain of being separated from family who chose bondage over freedom. They were left behind because they did not understand her calling or failed to see her for who she really was because of whatever impediments they were blocked by in their own psyche.

A question has been asked on many occasions, "Could the world handle it if Jesus were a woman?" While many say yes, history shows us that most women who held leadership roles in the context of world affairs were often without husbands or their husbands left them. There are many "isms." This is an example of the chains of sexism.

Another case is where a woman went to open a bank account in another country that she had moved to, and the bank told her that she could not open an account there because she was not born in that country. This is an example of having chains of nationalism.

Many people refused to support or vote for Barak Obama for president, not because of the issues or his ability to lead. This is an example of racism. A man goes in search of people, particularly women and uses force and bullying tactics to attempt to enslave them and force them to work for him while hitting them in the head with falsehood and lies as to break their spirit and uses his so-called wealth and their perceived condition to try to overtake them. This is an example of both sexism and materialism, not to mention abuse.

In your quest to remove the chains, you have to become brave to speak truth to power no matter sometimes how harsh it may be. Power is not the broken woman, who has been raped, robbed, spat on, used, abused, and misused. Yet empowered does she become when she recognizes who she is on all levels. At that point, she is able to bring her very best self to the forefront and walk gloriously in her truth. Balance is essential and the key to her balance is a Godly husband and man who understands who she is and what she is destined to become in God's eyes, not his own, then helps her to get there.

Gaining the courage to live freely is about cultivating your innermost feelings to experience joy, peace, happiness, and love. This comes from doing what you have always wanted to do. It is about fulfilling your dreams. There is nothing more profound than to give birth to your ideas and profit from what you love doing the most. You can experience real meaning in life when living in purpose. You do not have to wait on someone to give you permission. As a matter of fact if you do, you will find yourself in a rut and not living your dreams but rather living someone else's idea of you.

Don't get stuck doing someone else's job because you were afraid to fly and be you! You are able to pursue your real purpose in life and win at manifesting your dreams, which is your reason for being.

As you live in purpose you are free to be as creative as you choose. It's your option. So relinquish the need to ask permission to do that which you were born to do. If you were born to dance, why are you trying to organize a floor committee to change some tiles? If you are born with music in your heart, where is your song? If you were born to lead a country to victory, why are you following someone else's program? Mount up on your wings and fly!

It takes inner strength to walk freely because there are forces which naturally go against it. However, be courageous and remember that there are also forces which help in your elevation. The ascended masters are surrounding, protecting, loving, and guiding you on your journey. That, you must never forget. The only chains you have on are the chains you place on yourself; and limiting belief systems are also chains of bondage. Travel this journey we call life to live it, not to vicariously sit on the sidelines. Determine who you are and be courageous in living your truth.

To know what you have been born to do is an awakening experience. To actually do what you've been born to do is enlightenment. Be you and do you. Live your truth, not what someone else perceives your truth to be, but by what you know intuitively to be the truth of your soul. Be free, enjoy life, and move to allow others the same. Suppression and oppression are not characteristics of freedom. These are tactics that are used to hold up your progress, control you, and rob you of the most significant part of yourself, ultimately of your destiny.

Now, living freely does not mean you substitute good character. While good is relative, like everything else, living freely requires you to establish a set of ethics and principles by which you live by that does not compromise the integrity of someone else's right to free agency. The ability to pass the so often given character test depends not on who you know, it's about who you really are inside and how courageous you are to manifest that reality.

Presentation is everything. It is an outward expression of an internal attitude. What we believe is demonstrated by what we do. The key is to send out into the universe our very best and the very best comes back to us. There is a universal flow which exists, and as we connect to the higher and supreme source of all existence, we come to realize a creative power beyond anything we have ever known. Yes, we can establish universal peace where humanity can live together in harmony. We must think it, we must believe it, we must write it, we must speak it, and we must act upon it. It starts with each one of us. It's a decision and one only you can make for yourself. Yet, it is a decision that impacts the world. Freedom is learning to love and live being spectacularly you!

I am that I am, and that is a very colorful being: colorful meaning creative and I am not afraid to be gloriously, spectacularly, exquisitely, courageously me! Many people are born to do many things. So why not do the things you were born to do. That way the world is not deprived of something it desperately needs to be whole.

How dare you not be all of the wonderful and magnificent things that you really are? Let your light shine as bright as it will beam. A person in the dark, who is searching for light, never complains when light shines that it is too bright. Instead, they appreciate being able to see more clearly. Even jerks help you to shine brighter.

Inside of every human being is the potential to be phenomenally great. So recognizing one's greatness is pretty ordinary. However, attaining to greatness is extraordinary. Life experiences provide wonderful opportunities to learn and grow. Whatever you do, don't give up on yourself even though others may. Forge straight ahead, keep your head up. Know who you are and walk in the truth of who you are and what you are born to do!

Chapter 5

Enjoying the Beauty of Being Free

Many people view freedom as financial freedom only. Others will say that someone who says money isn't everything is usually poor. This depends on how you think and your orientation of mind. The truth is we need money to live in this world. Who does not want the material blessings that come with hard work and creativity? However, what must be understood is that you can have all the material possessions that you feel can help you be the most comfortable, but the truth is, if you do not have love in your life, then you really don't have a thing.

For some to be free is to have a huge credit line and the "power" to go purchase anything you like, when you like, and how you like. Yet, is that really freedom? Others feel that being surrounded by many people that are usually on the payroll is freedom. Is it really? I want you to think about what freedom really means to you. There is nothing like the awesome power of love. There is nothing greater than the power of love.

Let me tell you something. Many men have attempted to lay their wealth at my feet and my door, just for the honor of winning my love. Men have offered me the world, for the chance to pay all of my bills, for the chance to make me "famous," for the chance to spend just a little time with me and the chance to look at me or hear my voice a little longer. In their quest to capture my heart, they attempt to give me things that mean nothing above love and the source of the greatest love there is.

No one can buy the beauty and power of love for in this is the highest and most profound level of freedom. To be free is to love with all your heart, mind, and soul and have that returned to you in equal or greater measure is something that can only be comprehended through the experience of it. Love is free to all to have, but it must come from an open heart filled with love with only the highest intentions.

Being free is overcoming the bondage of your past to begin living in your truth. Being free is about doing what you love doing and having meaningful relationships built on a solid foundation of love and trust, and to gain the rewards of the work that you put out. Being free is about not having skeletons in the closet. Being free is about having that one moment in time knowing that you have found your destiny, then turning that one moment in time into a lifetime, then turning that into eternity.

Freedom is when you can truly look into the mirror and love who you are with all of your idiosyncrasies and not be concerned about how others judge you. It is living in your truth and being incredibly creative from the spirit of inspiration rooted in the power of love.

To enjoy the beauty of being free is to sing, dance, write, speak, or whatever your purpose is for the glory of the Ultimate source not worrying about having to "make" money to "survive." Now that is bona-fide and authentic freedom. The recognition that you have a birthright and that to walk with and in the authority of that birthright releases all the wealth and treasures of this world and beyond. There is no need to survive. You only have to focus on doing what you are born to do and live freely and what you need, want, and desire comes to you, including the material wealth that you are seeking. You just have to stay the course, not give up, and know that it will happen for you.

There is no greater love than that, there is no greater wealth than that, and there is no greater freedom than that. Enjoying the beauty of freedom is recognizing that you are wealthy beyond what any carnal man or woman can offer to get you to sell away your birthright. Walk in your purpose without fear of lack and experience the abundance flowing to you continuously.

About the Author

Atiya, founder of The Marriage Tree, has over the past 20 years, dedicated her life to honing her craft and, indeed, her calling – to empower, build and maximize human potential by affecting profound transformation in people's attitudes, perspectives and behaviors. She has been the catalyst responsible for inspiring countless people worldwide to realize their dreams and achieve joy, success and fulfillment in life.

Now she's bringing all her past experiences, edu-cation, and business-development skills from her considerable history as a speaker, author and life coach to focus on her core message: marital harmony ~ extended and profound.

Yes! It is possible to have an enduring relation-ship that is a positive and rewarding experience for both partners. But like anything of value, it requires fine-tuning and the willingness to learn to navigate the intricacies and subtleties of the changes any marriage encounters during its lifetime. Marriage is organic – it changes, evolves, grows - or like

many living things, without proper nurturing, it can deterio-
rate. But the good news is: it doesn't have to break down.
Building a history is a worthwhile, satisfying goal, as well as
a tangible legacy for your children.

Atiya is at once an optimist and a pragmatist. She's a
firm believer in the reality of a happy and satisfying long
term marriage. But she's no Pollyanna, having herself
encountered the vagaries of marriages over the past 21
years. She has come through them stronger and happier,
gratefully committed, and she can help you to achieve the
same result! She'll be the first to tell that what she's going to
show you won't be easy, but she's sure of one thing – it will
be worth it!

You deserve to live a life filled with mutual inspiration
and genuine respect. Atiya has the resources – intellectually
and empathetically - to guide you to fruitful solutions that
will not only positively-impact your relationship, but, as
importantly, will leave you personally empowered.

Also by Atiya

From Ordinary to Extraordinary

Purposeful Dating

Hidden Pearls

Petals of a Rose

Love is Not a Game

Overcoming the Pain of Losing a Mother

www.ingramcontent.com/pod-product-compliance
Lightning Source LLC
Chambersburg PA
CBHW071024040426
42443CB00007B/917